Animals A to Zoo

Written by Julie Lee and Jackie Northard
Illustrated by Kristine Kirkeby

Published by the Minnesota Zoo, 13000 Zoo Boulevard, Apple Valley, Minnesota 55124.

ISBN 0-9649808-0-

This book is lovingly dedicated to all children, especially Dylan, Daniel, Christopher, Emily; to all animals, wild and captive; and to the childlike imagination in all of us.

Amazing Animals

Bison Blowing Bubbles

Caribou Carrying a Canoe

Dolphins Dancing

Eagles Entertaining

Flying Fish

G g G g G g G g

Gibbons in Galoshes

Hedgehogs Hula Hooping

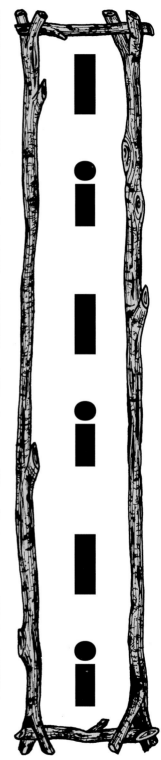

Iguanas Ice Fishing

June Bugs Jumping Rope

Komodo Dragons Kissing

L L L L
I I I I

Llamas in a Limousine

Moose Making Music

Northern Lights are Nice

Otters Eating Os

Prairie Dogs Playing Pinochle

Quills in a Quilt

Red Pandas Racing

Sharks Shoveling Snow

Tiger Trimming Toenails

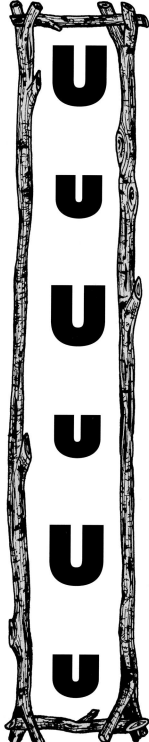

Unicornfish in Uniform

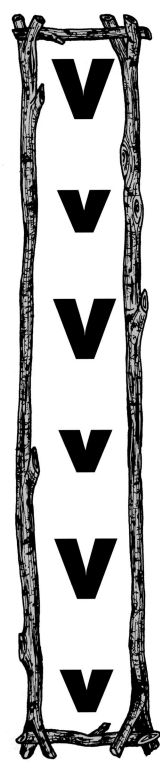

Vultures Visiting the Vet

Wolves Wrestling

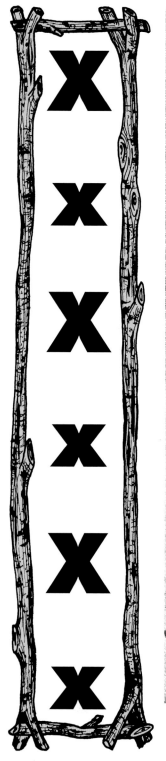

eXtra Busy Days

Youngsters Yawning

Catching Zzzzzzzzzs